BOTTOM IS BACK

For my dear friend
Nori Odoi

26 Jan 95

Also by Richard Moore

Poetry

A Question of Survival
Word from the Hills
Empires
The Education of a Mouse
No More Bottom (An Orchises Book)
Through the Keyhole

Fiction

The Investigator

Essays

The Rule that Liberates

Translation

The Captives of Plautus

BOTTOM IS BACK

*Let him renounce rhyme's fetters
and leave verse to his betters.
He thinks himself too grand,
this ass in fairyland.*

*This workman in the wood—
he'd love us if he could.
Then must we hear him rant
because he says he can't?*

Poems by
RICHARD MOORE

Prefatory Poem by
X. J. KENNEDY

ORCHISES WASHINGTON 1994

Copyright © 1994 Richard Moore

Library of Congress Cataloging in Publication Data

   Moore, Richard, 1927–
   Bottom is back / Richard Moore
      p. cm.
   ISBN 0-914061-43-7 : $11.95
   I. Title
PS3563.063B68 1994
811'.54–dc20   94-6557
                                  CIP

Manufactured in the United States of America

Published by Orchises Press
P. O. Box 20602
Alexandria
Virginia
22320-1602

G 6 E 4 C 2 A

for John Mella

Acknowledgments

The author wishes to thank the editors of the publications in which many of these poems first appeared:

Agni: "The Cinder," "Old Fools, Part III"
The Bridge: "The Bark"
Chronicles: "The Wife Beater's Punishment," "Rome," "Truth"
The Classical Outlook: "A Classics Scholar Views Her Second Husband," "Confession of an Old-Fashioned Historian," "The Interconnectedness of Things"
Drastic Measures: "One Tires of the Passing Scene"
The Epigrammatist: "Conversation Galante," "An Excuse Maybe," "A Heartening Message from Below," "A Machine for Everything," "The Old Poet," "Poetic Fashion"
The Formalist: "A Cultural Heavy," "To a Friendly Reviewer"
Kansas Quarterly: "In Praise of Old Wives"
Light: "Cultural Transplant," "The Devaluation," "Floral," "For a Feminist," "The Helicopter," "Malcolm," "Marital Nirvana," "On Receiving a Contract to Translate *The Iliad*," "Out of It," "Overheard at a Feminist Conference," "Personal Ad," "The Poet Finds Himself," "The Poet Laments the Decline of His Powers," "Suburb Song," "What's in a Name?"
Light Year '85: "On Coming to Nothing"
Mathematics Magazine: "The Last Duel"
Negative Capability: "Distraction on the Platform"
Plains Poetry Journal: "On Coming to Nothing," "Platonic"

Poetry: "On Coming to Nothing," "Pond Thoughts"
The Review: *Words And Images*: "The Maiden Aunt Variations"
Re-Publish: "The Bark," "The Heap"
Salmagundi: "The Heap," "In the Rough"
Sparrow: "For the Cold Night"

"Sharing the Onus" by X.J.Kennedy was first published in *Light*.

The author also wishes to acknowledge his indebtedness to the Djerassi Foundation and the Virginia Center for the Creative Arts, where some of the composition of this book happened.

Sharing the Onus

for Richard Moore

For sure, Dick Moore, what fate is worse,
    And are we not delirious
To wear the curse folks cast on verse
    Acerbic or unserious?

Some, for whom cuddling with the times
    Is chief *modus vivendi,*
Indict our rhymes for all known crimes
    Save trying to be trendy

And placing their respect in worms,
    Indignantly insist
That all Creation's vilest form's
    An epigrammatist.

Straight-faced as stuffed owls stuck on rods,
    They load up and besiege us
Poor rhyming clods with fusillades
    Of open verse egregious—

But let's not one iota veer
    From meter, craft, or candor
And yet aspire to hoist brown beer
    With Byron, Bierce, and Landor.

X. J. Kennedy

CONTENTS

	PREFATORY POEM	9
One:	**PENNY CANDY**	
	The Heap	15
	The Helicopter	17
	The Devaluation	19
	In the Rough	20
	The Old Poet	24
	A Heartening Message from Below	24
	The Last Duel [of a Mathematician]	24
	On Coming to Nothing	24
	The Cinder	25
	Out of It	27
	The Bark	28
Two:	**THE MAIDEN AUNT VARIATIONS**	
	The Maiden Aunt Variations	31
Three:	**OLD WIVES**	
	In Praise of Old Wives	49
	Distraction on the Platform	51
	Personal Ad	51
	Floral	51
	For the Cold Night	52
	A Classics Scholar Views Her Second Husband	53
	A Machine for Everything	53
	Marital Nirvana	53
	Credit in Unum	54
	Overheard at a Feminist Conference	56
	For a Feminist	56
	Platonic	56
	The Wife Beater's Punishment (with Commentary)	57

	What's in a Name?	58
	Conversation Galante	58
	The Poet Finds Himself	59
Four:	**OLD FOOLS**	
	Old Fools	63
Five:	**TRUTH**	
	The Poet Laments the Decline of His Powers	79
	Suburb Song	81
	Malcolm	83
	Cultural Transplant	84
	A Cultural Heavy	84
	An Excuse Maybe	84
	Confession of an Old-Fashioned Historian	85
	The Interconnectedness of Things	85
	On Receiving a Contract to Translate *The Iliad*	85
	Truth	86
	Rome	90
	Poetic Fashion	91
	To a Friendly Reviewer	91
	One Tires of the Passing Scene	91
	Pond Thoughts	92

One

PENNY CANDY

THE HEAP

All that you ever ask a tooth to do
        is chew,
and maybe (if you're wealthy, vain, and twitty)
        look pretty.

Why does it, then, like telescopes named "Hubble,"
        make trouble
and, losing all its vigor and its clout,
        fall out?

Perhaps the scientist can plumb this well
        and tell.
"It's just another case of entropy,"
        says he,

"Things (like bright colors mixed to muddy brown)
        run down.
It's happening throughout the universe,
        this curse,

so why not in (as east, west, north and south)
        your mouth?"
O sir, I feel, now that I've understood,
        so good.

With God's great compost heap I come to terms,
        whose worms
shall render me, dark, deeper than all hurt,
        to dirt.

All those who find that heap's creeping and crawling
          appalling—
it's like my tooth, sirs, wobbling in its socket.
        Don't knock it.

THE HELICOPTER

In summer
I like to see that hummer,
that helicopter, orange and seraphic,
hover
over
the traffic.

My love and I were once betrothed,
lying in darkness, half unclothed,
listening to it there
up in the air,
and I was glad my dearest never loathed
the questions that I popped her
under that helicopter.

Was it its chop, chop, chop,
that made her fling and flop?
Or were its whirring wings
symbols of subtler things?

Mortals who clog
in traffic jams,
honking below,
look up agog
where it flimflams
in the sun's glow,
for it knows more than they shall ever know
of where they'll go
and why they're there
in hot despair,

17

> grumbling, dour,
> frustrated, sour,
still inching homeward through the cocktail hour.

> It glimpses the Big Picture,
> each wreck, each traffic stricture,
> and talks to us below
> over the radio.

'Copter so bright, with oracles bewilderin'
> now my betrothed has seven children,
> > while still with clouds you mingle,
> > > blissfully single,
> a friend to man . . . Thou sayst:
"Get on with it! No time to waste!"
Though I stand still, my rotors are in haste.
> Though I look clean,
> I'm full of gas and grimes;
I've been rebuilt now thirteen times.
> Just a machine,
> I don't care what you're doing.
O mortal, leave me to my screwing."

THE DEVALUATION

Those wild Romantic boys
who could divine and dream
have picked up every theme
and eaten all our joys.

We lack their gifts, their poise,
their youth, their self-esteem.
We seethe, huff, blow off steam;
some say we just make noise.

When there was penny candy,
the kids picked pavements bare...
Look: pennies everywhere!

Beloved, fill the cup!
We who are old and randy—
come on, lez pick 'em up.

IN THE ROUGH

1

There in the clear
golfers pass;
in the rough here
a perfect sphere
buds in the grass.

The golfers' goal
is nothingness,
the hole.
I aim for less,
this solidness.

2

Off his aim,
he lost it here;
having no aim,
I have it here.

3

O plenitude of nature,
do you produce golfballs?

4

Father of noisy daughters, look.
A bright white testicle, lost.

5

They lie there nested, eggs.
These words are hatching from them.

6

One finds them best,
stirring nothing,
hopeless,
aware simply of every grassblade.
It's very difficult.

7

One needs golfballs.
It's so much easier to contemplate
something
than to contemplate
only.

8

To look for golfballs
is to protect oneself
from seeing too many other things.

9

In these woods are more poems
than golfballs.
Why do I look for the golfballs?

10

Leaves sprout
from an old stump.
The tree still grows
out of the ruin of itself.

11

To glimpse a poem, golfball,
sharpens the soul.

12

Exactly round,
they do not change,
only mud over.
Some get found.

13

Do these white spheres belong here?
Do I weed them out?

14

I keep them in a closet
in a box without a marker.
The closet is dark,
the box darker.

15

Autumn corrupts the woods.

In the morass of leaves
they lie, where rot encumbers,
unchangeable as numbers.

In each new age
things alter in the human brain.
Only the integers remain.

"We integers," said the golfball,
"without the human brain
would not exist at all."

I learned a clever proof today
by a man who is dust.

16

—What are you doing in there?
—Looking for golfballs.
—I wouldn't waste my time doing that.
—I wouldn't waste my time playing golf.
—I have to play golf. I'm an *addict*.
—Then you know why I look for golfballs.

17

I find what he has lost.
Who will find what I have lost?

18

When all this is over,
I will sell my golfballs to a golfer,
who will put them back where I found them.

THE OLD POET

The thunderstorm long since has passed.
    It couldn't last.
But still there's dripping in the night.
    I sit and write.

❖

A HEARTENING MESSAGE FROM BELOW

Though it's hot here, I grant,
I choose life—said the ant—
    Yea, though I live it
    under a trivet.

❖

THE LAST DUEL [OF A MATHEMATICIAN]

    Hector's paces
    were vector spaces.

❖

ON COMING TO NOTHING

Old friends, nearing senility,
we sit, every last prospect dim,
and think: The world was wrong about me. . .
but at least it was right about him.

THE CINDER

Employers need outwitting;
and so, instead of quitting—
costing them, understand,
forty or fifty grand,

I managed to get *fired*.
I call myself "retired,"
but, friends, I am a *fiery*
and passionate retiree.

Leaving the hurly-burly
of life and labor early,
crazier by the minute,
I gaze at those still in it

and feel a warm sensation:
my final conflagration.
Now busily and gaily
I ignite in verse daily

and flame out in my toil
like shining from shook foil
(who cares if I sound odd
and echo Hopkins' God?)

then shrivel to a cinder
among my *toten Kinder*.
Belinda, good and just,
watches me in disgust,

light-shedding, brightly orbed,
and says I'm "self-absorbed."
Unperked, unpaid—yea, pelfless—
I think I'm downright *selfless*,

dancing about and glowing
while the north wind is blowing.
Soon, mixing with that weather,
I'll vanish altogether.

OUT OF IT

End of the ride!
All off! . . . O, no!
Not yet! And so
undignified!

Retired? Say, "Died!"
Alright, I'll go—
angrily, though!
Friends gently chide,

"Why so appalled?
There's no more hurry
now, no more care."

No, and the bald
man need not worry
he'll lose his hair.

THE BARK

      A pox
on sexy joggers with their flowing locks
          and bouncing . . .
O God! I do believe they'd make a hound sing—
          and us:
I'll crouch and bark louder than Cerberus
          and damn
all who recall to me how old I am.

      Lords, ladies,
go lightly, lightly. Soon we'll jog in Hades,
          and there,
where bones are vapor and flesh thinnest air,
          no bark
disturbs the silence and the endless dark.

Two

THE MAIDEN AUNT VARIATIONS

THE MAIDEN AUNT VARIATIONS

Theme

My maiden aunt's
tomato plants
will never dance
without their pants.   *[Repeat with emphasis.]*

Variations

   1

That sounds to us
tautologous:
plants and their food
are always nude.

Only the best
of *beasts* get dressed,
and even they
don't stay that way

but keep on gripping
zippers and stripping
in every season
for some dumb reason.

2

Won't dance without
their pants? No doubt,
then, to some rhythm
they will dance with 'em.

With? O, my word,
Sir, that's absurd.
Whoever'd dance
with pairs of pants?

Though strong and proud,
he would be cowed
in the attempt: he
would find them *empty*.

3

O emptiness,
in my distress
you often haunt me,
echo me, daunt me.

For me you are
a darkened star:
collapsed, destroyed,
so full, it's void.

Through space it rushes,
catches and crushes
all in its path.
Image of wrath,

sweep through my inner
spaces, mad spinner!—
bottomless hollow,
destined to swallow

this whole sunned earth,
its madness, mirth,
its mountains, steeples,
and all its peoples.

4

A thought of Plato's
showed me tomatoes
clad in a mist.
I raised my fist,

"Hence, panaceas!
Empty ideas!
Metaphor clothing
fills me with loathing."

5

Well, come then, fetch up
your favorite ketchup
container, houser,
shaped like a trouser,

and think a minute
what fruit is in it…
This thought of bottles
was Aristotle's,

who said, "The ONE
won't feed you, hon'.
For life, one tucks
into the FLUX:

tomatoes, grapes,
losing their shapes—
transcend their losses,
dancing in sauces."

6

She no man's played in
is called a maiden.
That's why I can't
vouch for my aunt.

She might have carried
on, though unmarried,
with boxers, rowers,
tomato growers...

7

If auntie'd been
sexy and willing,
one men could win,
and not so chilling,

would her tomatoes
as if by pricks
of swords of Sato's,
have turned some tricks

and done deep deeds
by guile or chance
and dropped their seeds,
if not their pants?

8

My maiden aunt's
dead. Sweet romance,
I dare aver,
eluded her.

The crowds of suitors
in cars, on scooters,
prospective mates
who stormed her gates

drawn by her fruity
succulent beauty
and youthful glow,
left years ago,

dejected all—
the short, the tall,
Mercuries, Joves,
turned down in droves.

Hot lust annoyed them,
but she enjoyed them
and while they lasted
exercised, fasted,

to keep in trim
for Sir Right, him
astride his charger
who would enlarge her

with his deep surge in…
She stayed a virgin,
saddening, moping,
but always hoping,

never admitting
that her strange flitting
showed something near
disgust, or fear.

She played all sorts
of arts and sports—
piano, tennis—
to fight the menace,

but loved golf best.
She felt so blessed,
freed from all galls,
whacking those balls.

Also that tame
businessman's game
fit without strife
in her new life;

for as youth passed
she'd found at last
safety from sperm
in a law firm.

Competent, calm,
exuding balm—
yes, and a very
fine secretary,

elite or pica—
she rose up like a
well-hit golfball
into the squall,

responsibility.
With what agility
she sailed there, proud
and swift, through cloud,

thunder and wind,
so disciplined
and so adept,
directors wept

for joy to see
such industry,
keeping in hand
at her command

by sun and moon
a whole platoon
of female typers
fresh out of diapers

(which they were ready
with help from steady
trustworthy men
to fill again).

And she, still witty,
charming and pretty,
sensing her loss,
cleaved to her boss,

while he, alas,
as one who'd pass
in peace through life,
cleaved to his wife.

To have him thus
monogamous,
however, pleased
her, though it teased.

Strange how it comes
to spinsters, mums,
love's bitter bite:
Boss was Sir Right.

And so we add
right here the sad
gist of our song:
Sir Right was wrong,

who had no thought
for what he'd caught
without design.
There on his line

she hung, ignored,
yet daily bored
all with her stories
of Boss's glories.

And as the years
wore her, and fears
corroded ease
with injuries

imagined, real
(for one can feel,
losing one's sleep,
either as deep)—

witty and pretty
became just twitty.
She liked to touch
us, talked too much.

We heard her trips,
her fevers, grippes,
squirmed in those jails,
her endless tales.

The typers giggled;
the firm was niggled
in all its sectors.
So the directors

gave her a cruise
and all the booze
that she could hold.
Auntie'd grown old.

And she was pensioned
and never mentioned
there by the men
or "girls" again.

It would appall
to know what gall
this final shove
squeezed from her love

to drip on flowers
of her last hours.
I can think yet…
Let me forget.

I'll heave a sigh.
When did she die,
then? Last December?
I can't remember.

Is there no blame
here I might name?
Will no one bless
this emptiness?

    9

One maiden aunt
said in her youth,
"Tell all the truth,
but tell it slant."

10

Each anthill owns
a few sad drones
and just one queen.
Filling the scene,

all worker ants
are maiden ants:
infertile females
distilling dream ales

and other nectars.
They are the Hectors,
Bolivars, Caesars,
with mouths like tweezers—

the Newtons, Priestleys
among those beastlies,
who keep the hive
safe and alive.

It's called a nest?
We do our best,
the ants and I.
I don't know why.

11

In the lost time
before my prime
years freed my tongue,
sleeping among

relatives—gramp,
grandma—a camp
where summers bake
huts by a lake,

there, late one night,
lighting dim light,
thinking I slept,
my auntie crept

softly to bed,
and as I said,
I wasn't ready
for something heady

like that, that reared
as she appeared
with missing bodice,
turned to a goddess.

Auntie, I tell you,
I still can smell you,
touch you, and taste you—
though heavens waste you

as the earth did
and I stayed hid,
your beardless lover,
under his cover.

12

"Men are the maid-
en aunts of Being,"
the wild dogs bayed
in darkness fleeing.

"Taming the fire,
they tamed their being:
feeling, desire
in darkness fleeing.

"There in the night
where their skins glisten,
they crouch in fright,
in terror listen.

"Each, separate now
from all that is,
roots like a sow
and calls it his.

"Cursed is his art
and blind his seeing.
He stands apart
in darkness fleeing."

13

Then let us dream
in social trance
and let us seem
to fill our pants:

there softly lie
and try to bless,
tantalized by
their emptiness.

I tell you, coz,
sometimes we still it
simply because
we're fat and fill it.

14

Auntie, it's time
to tell you: I'm
your—and none saner—
living container,

your well-wrought urn,
for which I burn
—and where God stashes—
your lovely ashes.

And now I'm free.
Come dance with me.
Tomato plants
can also dance.

15

It's true, it's true!
To me, to you
sometimes unbidden
what long was hidden

in sleep, in trance
bares in a dance,
and freed from tether,
things leap together.

My maiden aunt's
tomato plants
will sometimes dance
without their pants.

Three

OLD WIVES

IN PRAISE OF OLD WIVES

Let her become my mate
and get me in her power
and save me from the fate
of Arthur Schopenhauer.

Cursing the common people, he
led a secluded life
and, hating women deeply,
grew old—and had no wife.

A young sculptress appeared,
disarmed, charmed, got his trust.
It happened as he had feared.
She carved his famous bust.

The portrait, thought by many
to show her adoration,
sold for a pretty penny
and made her reputation.

Together they rejoiced.
Her compliments were deft.
His glad old eyes were moist.
A month later, she left.

There was a power above her—
duty to art, she said.
There also was a lover,
and he was good in bed.

Poor Arthur pined away,
was buried in the spring.
People incline to say,
women were not his thing.

But is that *all* to say?
A good old jealous wife
keeps sculptresses at bay,
philosophers in life.

DISTRACTION ON THE PLATFORM

Beautiful in rebuttal,
    she's
a past master of subtle-
    ties.

❈

PERSONAL AD

My life's spontaneous, unforced.
    I love to mix and mingle.
Married three times, three times divorced—
    I guess that makes me single.

❈

FLORAL

Before affection sours,
    "say how you feel with flowers."
And when love dies, to express that,
    mail her a dead cat.

FOR THE COLD NIGHT

(his wife having become a lesbian)

    Under the blustery brunt
of winter, blankets soft and thick:
this whole warm bed is like a cunt,
    and I'm its throbbing prick.

    I revel in sensation.
I twist and stretch, and I plunge deep.
Plush presence! Luscious intimation!
    The end of each, sweet sleep.

    But similes break down,
and there's a difference in this:
my bed can't argue, spit, and frown,
    can't poison every kiss,

can't leave me naked and half dead
    to find another...*bed*.

A CLASSICS SCHOLAR VIEWS HER SECOND HUSBAND

Mirabile Dictu,
he got a prick too.

❊

A MACHINE FOR EVERYTHING

To make love to a robot
feels nice, I know, but
take care when you hug it
that you don't unplug it.

❊

MARITAL NIRVANA

Divorcees and divorcers shall divorce—
refine and rerefine their misery:
O pure elixer, quintessential source!
    There, where both genders fit,
having rubbed off all sign of sex, he, she
dissolve into the universal *it*.

CREDIT IN UNUM

To fill the moral void
when God Almighty dies,
some shall believe in Freud,
some in the Nobel Prize.
All-yielding, nothing loath,
Sibyl believed in both.

Her faith was eager, touching;
it made my heart glow warmer.
I *liked* to see her clutching
that holy man, the former,
but I could best get at her
by lashing at the latter.

"A Nobel Prize for *him*?
Why, Frost—like several fellows—
shines bright enough to dim
glimmers from twenty Bellows."
She, waking to a jury,
lept from the bed in fury.

Her kitchen pots went bang.
"Loving relationships
cannot survive," she sang,
"such jabs, such brutal quips."
I tried to soothe, finagle
at breakfast—a stale bagel.

I bit its crust and—tasting
truths that my crunching bruited—
departed, shriveled, wasting,
remorselessly uprooted,
who'd been a happy weed in
her lush and lovely Eden.

God of our winter chill,
why must You be so dead?
Had You been living still,
Sibyl had stayed in bed
and love, forgetting wrath,
bloomed in her primrose path.

OVERHEARD AT A FEMINIST CONFERENCE

Sisters, this may sound ominous,
but we all have a touch of the mom in us.

❧

FOR A FEMINIST

She would outcaesar Caesar—
I say in verse to tease her—
eliminate such sillies
as Homer and Achilles,
dress Milton in skirts, panties,
correct each sin of Dante's,
and, ready now to cast
ruin on all at last,
calls for the *termination*
of the whole *spermy nation*.

❧

PLATONIC

She is a woman of ideas, this Ms.
And the idea of her is better than she is.

THE WIFE BEATER'S PUNISHMENT

(with Commentary)

When he knocked out her tooth
(a beautiful incisor)
he lost his wife—plain truth:
he didn't recognize her.

Those verses sad and gory,
feminists brash and clubby,
began with a true story:
a wife thus bashed her hubby.

But *woman in a craze*
beats up her man in tales
lacks credence nowadays.
In fiction, thugs are males.

In life—I'll make a sonnet
and add—*don't depend on it.*

WHAT'S IN A NAME?

or

Stanley's Misunderstanding: A Tale of Marital Guilt

> In her talk—sense,
> current events,
> and such—occurred
> the striking word,
>
> *Uzbekistan.*
> Replied her man,
> "I can't say, Liz,
> who Becky is."

❊

CONVERSATION GALANTE

> "I know I've gotten fatter,"
> his wife confessed,
> "but how's my chest?"
> "I—" he said, "never flatter!"

THE POET FINDS HIMSELF

Wondering why she'd mate me
when she scorns, claims to hate me,
I wander with thoughts dark
and nasty through the park.
Light breezes brush the pond,
and in the sky beyond,
the sun is shining bright.
The trees guzzle the light;
each leaf, cleverly hung
on high, flicks like a tongue
and gulps it to the roots.
The baseball diamond hoots
when someone hits the ball.
There's something here for all.
O yes, and now I see
behind on the path three
incredibly fat-assed
joggers, waddling past.
And there on the pond—God A'
Mighty!—a whole armada
of ducks is on the loose,
led by a LONE MALE GOOSE,
who flew in last night from—from
wherever *gooses* come from.
To them who say that *geese*
is what I should say, "Cease!"
I say, "To me and you
your *geese* come two-by-two,
goose *lingam* and goose *yoni*
in paddling matrimony.
So *geese* have always done;
but that one's only one.

To clarify our uses,
his plural should be *gooses*."
O female—*goosies?*—eat your
hearts out for that creature,
who ranges free, untethered,
sleek and gaudy-feathered,
slender-necked and tall!
Yes! Something's here for all,
and all the signs agree,
goose is the guy for me.

Four

OLD FOOLS

OLD FOOLS

(For Knick: A Festschrift)

Part I

1

[What first drove him insane?
Did someone tweak his brain?
Dare we now go poking
into the naughty stroking
that wrinkled, pressed, and stretched,
and left poor Tristram tetched?
It was a prep school tetcher
made him a language lecher.
We won't (not that we ought)
say plainly what he taught,
what made him sympathize
and give Tristram a prize
for each masturbatory
poem, essay, story—
each prize a gentle shove
from an old fool in love
into that life of shame
known as the poetry game.]

2

O friends, friends, have you seen us?
I, like the Goddess Venus,
am sprung from love's mad foam.
I think I'll write a poem.
Out of your womb, dread brother,
[Tris cried] as out of mother
in blood and gore I came
in search of clapping fame.

(Clap-clap!—a dread disease,
punster, I hear you tease.
You gave me life, high grades—
no risks, no claps, no AIDS
in that lost carefree time
when such acts were a crime.)
But the cheers, the wild crowds
that lift us to the clouds,
our spirits soft as air
whistling everywhere,
high, high above the gritty
itches of the city...
I find no more, I fear,
than solitude right here,
a diet thin and fasty,
temperament growing nasty,
and attitudes that harden,
puttering in my garden.

3

Sanity comes unglued
in too much solitude,
which saturates all cheer
and pops the bright veneer.
Away, you pretty sheath!
Let's see what's underneath.
Just stuff of poorer quality,
jokes, quips, suchlike frivolity,
unworthy, undemanding
of critics' understanding,
the commonplace, the babble
delightful to the rabble,
thoughts reprobate and whoring,
nice people find so boring...
O, is there nothing vatic,
lyrical, or dramatic,
no naughty chorus dancing
in step with Freud's romancing?
Let the dread cauldron bubble!
No poison there, no trouble,
no game that's played for keeps
perks in its murky deeps.
The fire and stench of Hell
are now a little smell,
personal, sweetly tart,
and harmless as a fart.

4

A woman in your life,
mistress, tart, or wife—
a wise policy: it'll
settle your wits a little
or maybe stir them up—
certainly fill the cup,
both mythical and real,
that washes down the meal
of your life's cooked endeavor
with spirits, whines—whatever.
She has too many joys in you
(though sore tempted) to poison you.

Observers, though, can tell
it hasn't worked too well
as I amidst my nurses
sit scribbling these verses.
(Really it's just one nurse—
no harem. What a curse!
She answers in a huff:
"At your age, one's enough."
At *our* age, dear, one hates,
one's love evaporates,
yet one keeps getting randy.
I want another handy.)

Part II

1

And thus to bodies fated,
in which, incarcerated,
with naughty flesh uprisen—
come, let's away to prison!
We'll con the latest fads,
parody slogans, ads,
be lover, sister, brother,
and understand each other.
I'll copy you, sweet copier!
Ah, language, ever sloppier,
won't float us, won't uplift...
off into depths we drift,
lone paddlers, lost in mists,
pure selves, sad solipsists.

2

Some critics—testy birds!—
talk of "worn-out" words,
like "metaphor," like "taste."
O souls unzipped, unlaced,
playing at hide-and-seek
off in that chintzy clique
you joined—and pay your dues:
words aren't like old shoes
on dumps, pecked by you vultures.
Words are like yoghurt cultures.
With proper care and brewing,
and luck, they keep renewing,
ripening, growing—yum!—
wonderfully flavorsome.

Homeric bards, who sang
of yoghurt's mystic tang
before they left the scene,
can tell you what I mean—
men who maintained unslurred
life in the common word,
so listeners in the wood
heard it and understood;
men long in the past tense,
who sang Sir Patrick Spence,
Edward, The Baffled Knight,
and after bloody fight,
love's groves full softly mossed—
and God knows what's been lost.

3

Strange world, deep Academe,
dry myth, fantastic dream—
where a grad school "B-"
like Circe can enswine us.
Our goddess! See: we dress her
in robes, a full professor,
and, risking laughter, odium,
plop her on the podium,
and, sitting in the pews,
we eat her dead reviews,
catch creatures out of Hell free,
flying from her belfry,
her nonsense on the wing,
her Keats, each batty fling,
her rots, her moldy yeasts...
we chew, and turn to beasts.

Ah, long before she swished it,
deep down we must have wished it—
this idol come to bless
and hide our emptiness,
our clay spirit, numbed mind.
Pope's Dullness here enshrined,
whose Yawn protects the Nation
from joy, wit, inspiration—
come! Chase the poets hence!
They joke, sometimes make sense.
They open ear and eye.
Take me, dear, let me die,
swallowing Ammons; bury
me deep in gray Ashbery!

4

Here round about our Babel,
"Insanity's a label
to which many are liable,
but Knick was certifiable"—
so said a modern critic,
once famous, now arthritic,
whose classes I'd attended,
that trudged, carefully trended...

O Knick, you crazy devil,
you just wouldn't stay level:
in *your* classes hubbub,
mermaids in your bathtub;
yet in the laughs you triggered,
no mocks, and no one sniggered.
Thick-spectacled, blear-eyed,
somehow you terrified.

Marriage a secret mess,
your wife—"an authoress,"
wiser than you, all said—
restraining, only fed
the need to mock, lash, rave,
that weighed you to your grave,
a monster at the end.
No one can buck a trend.

Yours were my father's years.
Strange how death endears!
The honor that I give him
fades now. You outlive him.

Part III

1

Night ends; each morning brings
pleasure of touching things.
Fingers commune with fact
with skill age leaves intact,
enhances even: long
practice tunes the song
that the quick muscles sing,
and keeps us functioning
when all, all seems bereft—
as those days my wife left,
those huge first days when I,
everything gone awry,
all things in senses' range
intolerable and strange,
no firmness, wits not holding…
put up the kitchen molding.
Blessing, half understood—
that when I handle wood,
tools, something to be made,
all inner torments fade—
consciousness yoked to seeing
new things come into being.

Thus, love into rage lapsing,
the whole family collapsing
on floors above, old fools
in cellars fuss with tools.

2

Nursing my dear remorse,
one day on the golf course,
walking barefoot in jeans
down fairways, over greens—
that sunny afternoon a
funny dark man from Poona
(he said) thought we should meet.
He had observed my feet.
Toeing grass, gravel, loam,
they made him think of home—
no sunnier, more windy a
region in all of India—
where he grew, munched his mum's
pooris and pappadums.
There many people choose
to walk without their shoes
(and there, also, are many
so poor they haven't any)
and feel the hills, bogs, knolls
rub into their soles.
When skin and the world meet,
before hands, come the feet,
and both, it's clear, attain
man's state before his brain—
the story clearly told
by fossil men of old.

And such my own odd story:
how a conservatory
took all my teaching years.
People ask: "What endears—
whiling your life away
in such a place?" I say—
but no one understands—
musicians use their hands.
One trusts, thoughtlessly flings
into the play of things.
The droll merry-go-round
of the mind touches ground.

To whom shall I bequeath 'em,
my feet? No one could see them,
except the man I mentioned,
his mind rightly dimensioned.
Travelers see strange sights;
all's oddity, delights.
No longer formulaic,
accustomed, and prosaic,
all fascinates, intrigues,
desperately fatigues.
Hence natives, those who fit, 'll
observe so very little.

None noticed my bare feet,
I'd noticed. That was neat:
thus to progress unseen
over the park and green
where no one would molest me,
none honor me, none test me
for wickedness, enormity,
frivolous unconformity.
I'd had my honoring
from Knick, and felt its sting.
But now this man, as fated,
this Knick reincarnated,
had seen me once again.
He said: Indian men
after adulthood's varied
duties—their fathers buried
and their own inundation
in marriage, generation,
drenched in their struggles, rage—
climb out on dry old age,
give back earth's tawdry goods,
retire into the woods
where the wild beast trods,
and there joke with the gods.
And finding all things risible,
thus he becomes invisible,
springs out of life's sad cage,
empty, the perfect sage.

3

The sun's gone, and they're dark,
the golf course and the park.
An airliner thunders, jars,
roars past the planet Mars
and horribly in tune
heads for the setting moon.
I sit in snow. I'm old.
My bottom's getting cold.
The world we ventured from
lingers this evening. Come,
let's join the unseraphic
flash and fume of traffic
and the life—no, not pretty—
and nonsense of the city.

Five

TRUTH

THE POET LAMENTS
THE DECLINE OF HIS POWERS

Neath covers
met,
young lovers
get

their pleasures
still.
Their measures
fill.

Each scribbles
well
what sibyls
tell

while, raging
here
at aging
near,

with blightings
numb—
my writing's
come

a cropper.
Youth
could hop her
—Truth—

could dandle,
stir,
and handle
her

as spirits
led.
It's sere, it's
dead,

my talent.
Wits,
ungallant
twits…

O wimp, O…
spent!
I'm impo-
tent.

SUBURB SONG

Come live with me!
We'll spread the brie,
guzzle the wine, smoke dope,
and give up hope
for modern man's
estate
that fetters, bans
what's great
from his life of ease,
and fosters grubs and fleas.

We'll cultivate
curious herbs
and, resting from our labors
in posh suburbs,
we'll contemplate
our vile
upwardly mobile
neighbors.
Their life of ease
suits them, those grubs and fleas.

The one firm rule
in suburbs posh is:
when snow is falling, you'll
pull on galoshes,
and thus, all faring
in rubber
like great whales, bearing
their blubber
through seas of ease...
Listen, you grubs and fleas:

      The heroic past
      has passed at last
into a moral slum,
       and life's become
      a stuttery
          boast
      over buttery
          toast.
      A life of ease…
eat it, you grubs and fleas!

MALCOLM

His eye flashes,
his tooth bares.
Down the stairs
wildly dashes

mad Malcolm.
Silly nerd!
He's just heard
the mail come.

Strangest of chaps!
Loosely walled
angers pent,

he flaps, flaps.
That's why he's called
The Malcolm Tent.

CULTURAL TRANSPLANT

You'd move to Boston, Sir? Not murder, rape, nor rob here,
    but get an academic job here?
You're a household name, then—a prized, advertised bore
    who can take on the faddish tough
    and can outfashion and outfad 'em?
To be, Sir, an accomplished intellectual whore
        is not enough.
    You have to be a famous *madam*.

❧

A CULTURAL HEAVY

        For all his failings, he
        is an exquisite balance:
arrogance, bad manners, hypocrisy
        compensate lack of talents.

❧

AN EXCUSE MAYBE

"You were dishonest, lied,
    wrote hamily."
"I had to feed," he cried,
    "my family."

CONFESSION OF AN OLD-FASHIONED HISTORIAN

I'm an elitist, love art—O, a sinner!—
and don't care what the peasants ate for dinner.

❁

THE INTERCONNECTEDNESS OF THINGS

"You can't hope," his confessor
said solemnly to Daryl,
"to be made full professor.
Oil's *forty bucks* a barrel."

❁

ON RECEIVING A CONTRACT TO TRANSLATE *THE ILIAD*

Wise up, my boy! Give up the hell
of writing books you'll never sell,
and learn to take naughty delight
in selling books you'll never write.

TRUTH

(A Political Analysis)

"What's truth?" asked Pontius Pilate,
ever prepared to revile it,
"What's truth, you tramps and hags?"

"I know!"
said the wino,
hung with wretched rags.
"Truth is many-gowned.
She dresses for our sakes...
    but it's booze what makes
    the world go 'round.
Just look—look hard if you dare.
Continents here and there
soaking and eroding,
volcanos belching, exploding...
but mostly it's under covers—
oceans like gushy lovers—
mostly the earth's *all wet*.
What's it want then? *To forget*!
Iss' jus' like me an' Vivian.
All we want's oblivion."

But here, rolling eyes aloft,
one stood, politely coughed—
so elegant, so correct!—
and thus, commanding respect
and silence from every man
and woman there, began:

"I report to you, friends, that we—
that is, my colleagues and me…"

The crowd heard Pilate cry,
"You mean, *my colleagues and I!*
If you're going to whine and yammer,
do it with decent grammar!"

"My friends, my true assoc*iates,*
allied to me in their fates…"

"They lied to you?" Pilate inquired,
"Those friends you probably hired—
what kind of friends were those?
You talk too fancy. Speak prose!"

"My colleagues formed a committee
of the best minds in the City,
experts, fortune-gainers,
nationwide entertainers—
all those by whom truths are uttered."

"Boobs, jackals," Pilate muttered.
"After meetings around the Nation,
ten years' deliberation
at many a posh resort,
though official neglect…"

                                   "Make it short!"
cried Pilate.

                "Well, then—raising
no questions about the phrasing

and creating the false impression
of a shallow, debate-free session—
we all in due course agreed
that *Truth is much in need*."

"That all?" Pilate asked, "—in ten *years?*"

"O no! We resolved amid cheers—
ecstatic that, cleverly gleaning
our dictum's ulterior meaning—
that the duty should fall on us—
resolved—such claps—thunderous!—
that *Truth needs a father-confessor
to toilet-train and dress her.*"

A mechanic stood up in rage.
"This jerk thinks he's a sage.
Ban him from the City!
He's telling us Truth is sh—y."

Pilate breathed, "How I love these greasies!
Give them a whiff of feces,
and they'll outshout any crowd."

"My friend," he said aloud,
"thanks for your thoughtful words,
that lay bare these, these…"

                        "T—s!"

"…let's call them *stagnant pools*
in the *morass* of our schools.
But we'll keep them among us, I think—
so we won't forget how they *stink*."

"And so *you'll* smell nice by comparison
and stay in control of the garrison,"
shouted the happy mechanic—
who'd become, Pilate saw, too manic.
So the police appeared,
and as the crowd had feared,
doctors put him in chains
(and, a month later, beat out his brains).
And the crowd, with his strangled curse
in their ears, began to disperse,
and Pilate, too, strode from the scene.

The drunks remained on the green.

ROME

Stability at last: the Empire.
Automatons control the Government,
sentimentalists the intelligentsia,
those with imagination nothing.

POETIC FASHION

Always it changes—rhyme to rhymeless,
then back to rhyme. Is nothing timeless?
No seed there, no surviving kernel?
Stupid ...*stupidity*'s eternal.

❉

TO A FRIENDLY REVIEWER

Praise for my essay—thanks! You know I need it.
So I shan't quibble that you didn't read it.

❉

ONE TIRES OF THE PASSING SCENE

O Lord, come soon and get
me. Better your sweet clover
of nothingness than this new set
of nothings taking over.

POND THOUGHTS

1

As when into still water a stone drops
and disturbs peace, but ripple-circles spread
and all is calm again where the stone sinks:
so would I like to speak among my friends.

2

Why storm? Only the calmness of the trees
is mirrored in the pond; rage of the wind
will stir the trees and pond beyond reflection.

What is reflection but the branches blurred?
How can the water sense its depth unless
waves rise, branches their strength unless they howl?

3

This calm puddle, protected from the pond
by a thin ridge of sand, rinsed with the waves,
stays at the pond's level, which isn't level,
but humped and tossed. It seems a mystery—
something to do with seepage through the sand—
how the pool does it. As for keeping calm
while the great pond sways grandly up and down—
that it achieves simply by being small.
It is so quiet now that it seems empty—
just bare, wet bottom, clear in the sunlight,
trivial—but we need this nothingness,
this smooth and lucent zero here, to show
what those great positives and negatives,
rolling upon each other there, add up to.

4

The stones that skip scarcely disturb the water;
the ones that make great splashes merely sink—
to air and the smooth water unresponsive.
Worn ones go best—dipping so deftly down.
As men who, touching death before they vanish,
graze on it gaily, seem to feel no fear,
they seem to fly, touching a path of ringlets,
then let you glimpse their stillness one last time,
sliding a little, out into deep water...
It's not the same silence when they have gone.

5

The twinkling amber water in the twilight,
when the wind dies, how suddenly subsides.
Petulant waves that ruled the afternoon,
nowhere. Diminishing and looped with land,
their shallow ghosts pass faintly shore to shore,
as silent and evasive as the shadows.
And yet, though the reflections reappear
of dark foliage, shore lights, amber sky,
the water swarms with palpitation still,
as if remembering the afternoon,
foamy and gusty, full of iron whitecaps.
It takes the smoothness of a flight of ducks
to know the dream is over, the calm real.